THE ANGEL TREE

THE ANGEL TREE

THE LORETTA HINES HOWARD COLLECTION OF

EIGHTEENTH-CENTURY NEAPOLITAN CRÈCHE

FIGURES AT THE METROPOLITAN MUSEUM OF ART

LINN HOWARD AND MARY JANE POOL

PHOTOGRAPHS BY ELLIOTT ERWITT

ALFRED A. KNOPF   NEW YORK / 1984

All quotations from the Bible are from the Authorized (King James) Version.

Quotation from Olga Raggio, <u>Metropolitan Museum Bulletin</u> No. 24, 1965–66,

by permission of The Metropolitan Museum of Art.

Copyright © 1965 by The Metropolitan Museum of Art.

Library of Congress Cataloging in Publication Data

Howard, Linn, 1932–

The angel tree.

Bibliography: p.

1. Crib in Christian art and tradition—New York (N.Y.)

2. Howard, Loretta Hines—Art collections. 3. Christian

art and symbolism—Private collections—New York (N.Y.)

4. Metropolitan Museum of Art (New York, N.Y.)

I. Pool, Mary Jane.   II. Title.

N8065.H66 1984   704.9'4853'094573   84-47748

ISBN 0-394-53972-9

ISBN 0-394-72648-0 (pbk.)

Manufactured in Italy

First Edition

GRAPHIC CREDITS

Production: Ellen McNeilly

Design: R. D. Scudellari

Mechanicals: Francine Kass

Compositor: Haber Typographers

Printer & Binder: Amilcare Pizzi

FOREWORD

For over two decades, thanks to Loretta Hines Howard, the brilliantly lit Christmas tree bedecked with eighteenth-century Neapolitan angels and cherubs has provided a point of radiance in the vast stillness of the Medieval Hall at The Metropolitan Museum of Art. For young and old, for all who cherish the nostalgia and excitement of the Christmas season, the adornment and illumination of the tree is a glorious event. An awesome and wondrous sight, the tree has a sculptured base, a landscape in which exquisitely fashioned figures re-enact the joyous events that marked the Nativity. We see the three magi, dressed in sumptuous robes and surrounded by their lavish entourages and noble beasts of burden. We see the travelers and townspeople who thronged to Bethlehem; and in the center, flanked by the graceful figures of Mary and Joseph, we finally view the diminutive form of the Child, lying peacefully on a nest of straw. Our eyes do not rest, as one figure leads us to the next, and we marvel at the masterful craftsmanship of form and at the infinite care taken with each individual's face and gesture.

Most of the figures in the Loretta Hines Howard collection were once part of the famous Catello collection in Naples. We are indeed grateful to her for this splendid gift, which has imparted so much beauty and joy to Museum visitors through the years. It is a tribute to its creation that the impact is never diminished as time goes by; the crèche never fails to cast a spell of enchantment over each of us. I should also like to thank Linn Howard, Loretta Hines Howard's daughter, for continuing the work of her mother and for giving so much of her time and care to the installation each year.

PHILIPPE DE MONTEBELLO
Director, The Metropolitan Museum of Art

I / *According to Saint Luke, it was an angel who told Mary she would give birth to the Infant King. At The Metropolitan Museum of Art in New York, the joy of that Nativity is celebrated each year with a special exhibit of eighteenth-century Neapolitan crèche figures —a giant blue spruce encrusted with man's earthly image of angels and encircled with colorful figures enacting the wondrous events at the manger.*

The small crèche figures (the tallest reaches no more than twenty inches) number nearly two hundred. Each one is a treasured work of art. Their flexible bodies are made of hemp, tow, and wire, their arms and legs of beautifully carved wood. Their heads, exquisitely sculpted of terra cotta, are polychromed in celestial hues or the colors of all the peoples of the earth. They pose and gesture in expectation and adoration. All turn toward the Babe in a setting of columns probably inspired by those of the Temple of Castor and Pollux in the Roman forum —a surprising placement, meant to dramatize the triumph of Christianity over paganism. To see the crèche and tree in the Metropolitan's Medieval Sculpture Hall, in front of the Spanish Choir Screen from the Cathedral of Valladolid, is to experience all the fantasy and realism, mysticism and earthiness, grandeur and intimacy that the Christmas season inspires.

Re-creating the happenings at the crib, or <u>presepio</u> as it is called in Naples, is one of the most tender and enduring Christmas traditions. From the beginning the Nativity was celebrated in literature and art, music and liturgical drama, but it took some time for the idea to develop three-dimensional form. There is a touching legend about Saint Francis of Assisi, the poetic and compassionate man whose love of children and animals may have led to a most unusual Christmas in the Italian village of Greccio in 1223 . It is told that to create a second Bethlehem all men could understand, Saint Francis placed an ox, an ass, and some sheep in a mangerlike setting with an infant on a bed of straw. When the people came for midnight Mass, they were astonished at the sight and deeply moved. To some, when Saint Francis lifted the child into his arms, he seemed to waken, smile, and raise his little hand in blessing.

There are many accounts of early re-creations of the Nativity in crèche form in church writings and the publications of art historians. And there is a language to be learned. The expression "rocking the child" describes a religious practice in the middle ages of rocking a wooden infant in a cradle. The term "Bethlehem" refers to a group of stationary figures presented in a framed case. "Crèche," now a universal term, is a French word from the low Latin cripia, which means crib. In German crèche is Krippe, in Spanish, presebre. In Italian a three-dimensional, realistic depiction of the scene at the manger is a presepio. An intimate grouping of the Holy Family is often called a mistero.

Through the ages, whether the figures of the crèche numbered three or several hundred, simple craftsmen and highly skilled artists used a myriad of materials to fashion them—marble, wood, terra cotta, straw, cork, paper, wax, glass, ivory, and precious metals set with corals, pearls, and the rarest jewels. For example, marble figures by Arnolfo di Cambio were placed (c. 1291) in the Presepio Chapel in the church of Santa Maria ad Presepe (now Santa Maria Maggiore) in Rome, and after 1311 there were polychromed wood carvings of the Nativity in the nunnery of Santa Chiara in Naples. In 1344, Margaretha Ebner of the Dominican order wrote in her "Revelations" that she received from Vienna a Christ child in a cradle with four little golden angels. In 1489, the Bishop of Burgundy gave to his cathedral in Utrecht a reliquary-Bethlehem of gold, enamel, and jewels. The reflection of the jewels on the ceiling of the stable setting represented the Heavenly Light.

In the sixteenth and seventeenth centuries, constructing and displaying Christmas crèches was an important devotional practice of the Jesuits, which they took with them to the far corners of the world. Jesuit missionaries in Canada wrote in 1642 that their Christmas crèches were a great success with the American Indians.

The passion for presepi spread from the churches into houses and palaces. In 1567 the Duchess of Amalfi's inventory showed some one hundred sixteen figures, angels, and animals, including the Virgin with a unicorn. They were stored in two great chests and brought out every Christmas to be used in elaborately staged Nativity scenes. In 1580, a Bavarian princess wrote to her brother who was reigning in Munich, asking for articulated crèche figures dressed like fine dolls. By the time Don Carlos of Bourbon became King of Naples in 1734, crèche making was a national preoccupation. His own royal crèche was said to number some five thousand, nine hundred fifty figures.

Ferdinand IV, who acceded to the Neapolitan throne in 1759, created crèche figures with his own hands. His Queen, Maria Carolina, and her ladies delighted in sewing costumes that imitated their own fanciful rococo clothes, taking the greatest care with the tiny trimmings and accessories. Rustling silks, brocades, ribbons, and laces were woven with miniature designs to just the right scale. Even the figures representing the country people were dressed in homespun, leather, sheepskin, and other authentic fabrics.

Nesta de Robeck, in <u>The Christmas Presepio in Italy</u> *(Florence, 1934), paints a lively picture of* <u>presepio</u> *fervor in Naples at this time: "...It is said that four hundred Neapolitan churches annually set up their Presepio and many private houses too had their own 'Bethlehem' on which the owners spent vast sums of money, encouraged to do so by a famous preacher, Padre Rocco, who made the Presepio his particular object of devotion. His influence was enormous....Advent was spent in a frenzy of preparation and Christmas became a social event with people rushing from house to house, church to church, visiting, admiring, criticising each other's Bethlehem. Often the Presepio occupied the whole floor of a house, sometimes even the whole house, different scenes being represented in different rooms and concerts of appropriate Nativity music held in honour of any distinguished guest."*

Samuel Sharp, a British surgeon and visitor to Naples, recorded his experience of this spectacle in his <u>Letters from Italy</u> *(London, 1767): "...What renders a Presepio really an object for a man of taste, is the artful disposition of the figures, amidst a scenery of perspective, most wonderfully deceitful for the eye. A certain merchant has one on top of his house, where the perspective is so well preserved, that, by being open at one end, the distant country and mountains become a continuity of the Presepio, and seem really to be a part of it....”*

II / *Some of the most extraordinary crèche figures made in Naples in the eighteenth century are in the Loretta Hines Howard collection at the Metropolitan Museum. It was the great beauty and inspirational quality of such figures that led Loretta Howard to start her collection. Her eye for antiques and her interest in religious art began early, on family trips to museums and churches in Europe. In 1924, just before her marriage to Howell Howard, her mother found a small eighteenth-century Neapolitan crèche at Marshall Field's in Chicago and gave it to the bride for her new home in Dayton, Ohio. During her European honeymoon she looked for figures to add to the crèche and began the collecting that would become an important spiritual and artistic focus of her life.*

Loretta Howard was a prolific painter who studied with Robert Henri. After her husband's death in 1937, she moved with their four children to New York, to be near the center of the art world. She painted professionally and had several successful gallery shows. Her home was filled with art and artists. Friends poured in for family celebrations, especially Christmas, when the house was elaborately decorated and her crèches were displayed.

Through the years Loretta Howard searched for crèches to add to her collection and to give to family and friends. In 1949 she gave a noble crèche of eighty figures with architectural background to the Benedictine monastery of Regina Laudis, in Connecticut. The crèche had been made for Victor Amadeus, the King of Sardinia, and was presented to him in 1720, the year of his coronation. In 1962 Mrs. Howard was invited by President and Mrs. Kennedy to arrange a crèche at the White House,

and she continued to work with the White House throughout several administrations. In 1972 she gave a particularly splendid crèche to the Albright-Knox Art Gallery in Buffalo, in memory of her friend Helen Northrup Knox.

A highlight of Loretta Howard's collection, a crèche called "The Adoration of Angels," was exhibited in Paris in 1952 and brought to her attention by Francis Henry Taylor, who was then Director of the Metropolitan Museum. The owner of the "Adoration" was Eugenio Catello, a noted collector in Naples with whom Loretta Howard had been corresponding for several years, after an introduction by the famed art historian Dr. Rudolf Berliner. This crèche contained figures of the finest quality — thirty angels of exceptional beauty made it very desirable. Following three years of letters back and forth, the sale of the "Adoration," which represented three generations of Catello family collecting, was arranged.

Through their correspondence Loretta Howard had become very attached to Eugenio Catello, and she arranged a visit to Naples just to see him. She wrote: "I was met by an interpreter as I spoke no Italian. He took me to Mr. Catello's house where I was greeted by two very serious young men and a lovely young woman, all in deep mourning. They told me they were Mr. Catello's children and that he had just died. I was very shocked and quite spontaneously asked what had caused his death. They told me, 'joy!' I thought there must be some misunderstanding in the language, so I asked how that could be, and they told me this tale. Some years before, Mr. Catello's father had sold a magnificent crèche to the artist Sert. Mr. Catello heard that Sert was dead so he wrote to his widow in Paris to see if he could buy back the crèche. He never heard from her and then found out that she, too, had died. He was determined to locate the crèche. With the greatest difficulty, he finally found it and discovered it was in perfect condition as it had never been unpacked. He was so overcome with joy, he died. Many of the figures added to the Metropolitan crèche are from this collection."

When the "Adoration" arrived from Italy in 1955 without a traditional architectural background, Loretta Howard devised a way to put the figures into the family Christmas tree with angels swirling up to the top star. The effect was spectacular and was greatly admired. Robert Hale, her teacher at the Art Students League and a curator at the Metropolitan Museum, suggested to James Rorimer, the Director, that he ask Loretta Howard to re-create her angel tree at the Museum. And so she did, in 1957 and 1958. After similar exhibitions at the Albright Gallery in Buffalo in 1962 and 1963, and at the Detroit Institute of Art in 1964, she gave the "Adoration" to the Metropolitan for its permanent collection. In 1965 she assembled the first glorious display, which has delighted and inspired millions of visitors. It is the way in which Loretta Howard combined the Neapolitan Nativity with the Northern European Christmas tree—towering tree and encircling figures, glowing lights and joyous music—that makes it a work of art pleasing to the spirit and the senses.

In an article about the collection published shortly after the acquisition, Olga Raggio, Chairman of the Department of European Sculpture and Decorative Arts at the Metropolitan, says: "By far the largest group of figures in the Howard crèche is made up of a host of delightfully dimpled cherubs, delicately modeled like biscuit figurines, and some fifty large and elegant angels. These, clad in swirling pastel draperies, their hair knotted by a mystical wind, their cheeks flustered by a sweet celestial emotion, are seen swinging their finely chased silver-gilt censers or suspended in adoration. Did these heavenly creatures once belong perhaps to a famous crib set up every Christmas, until 1826, by the De Giorgio family, which had an extraordinary glory of angels that the people flocked to admire? We will never know for sure.

"Stylistic comparisons with many signed figures in the collections of Naples and in a documented crèche in the Bavarian National Museum in Munich suggest that about half of the Howard angels should be credited to the best late eighteenth-century masters: Giuseppe Sammar-

tino (1720–1793), well-known for his monumental sculptures in marble and in stucco, his pupils Salvatore di Franco, Giuseppe Gori, and Angelo Viva, and Lorenzo Mosca (d. 1789), who was employed at the Royal Porcelain Factory at Capodimonte and as stage director of the Royal Christmas Crib.

"In the central group of the Holy Family—the Mistero, as Neapolitans used to call it—the noble and tender figures of Mary and Joseph, who hover over the Babe lying in a manger, are also modeled and carved with exquisite care. They are attributed to Salvatore di Franco, who is mentioned by contemporary sources as one of the best presepio sculptors of the time. Next are the three magi, splendidly attired in long cloaks of silk embroidered with silver, gold, and sequins, topped with simulated ermine capes, their costume perhaps inspired by the colorful garb worn by the Knights of San Gennaro on the yearly festival in Naples. They approach the Divine Infant, their faces glowing with expressions of tender awe and piety, marvel or mystical expectation, gesturing with their delicate, nervously expressive hands.

"Behind the magi come the mingled crowd of brightly dressed, exotic travelers, who symbolized the homage rendered by all nations to the Divine Child: there are Mongols and Moors mingled with Turks and Circassians, advancing on horseback or on foot, carrying their colorful trappings, banners, and lances, followed by their camels, attendants, and dogs. It is in this section of the presepio that the imagination of patrons and artists, free from literal fidelity to the Scriptures, fascinated by exotic costumes and types, gave itself full rein and indulged in the wildest flights, in a vein that reminds us of the world of the Turqueries and 18th-century opera and ballet rather than sacred drama. To these figures belong some of the most elaborate accessories, finely chased and gilded scimitars and daggers, silver baskets, and purses, all miniature masterpieces executed by Neapolitan silversmiths and other craftsmen.

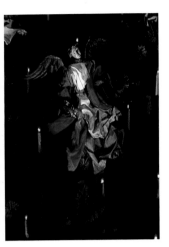

"A sure theatrical instinct presided over the creation of a Neapolitan Christmas crèche. The world of the exotic was counterbalanced by the more homely world of humble shepherds and simple folk, who act out their emotions and speak the language of the heart. We see some of the shepherds, clad in rough sheepskin clothes, awakened from their sleep by the Angel of the Lord, dazzled by the light that suddenly breaks through the night or bemused by the celestial music that fills the heavens, their faces reflecting their feelings with pulsating vitality and truth. Nothing is conventional here, and the 18th century has hardly left us more lively and natural portraits than these. Academically trained artists, sometimes well-known as porcelain modelers—like Francesco Celebrano, to whom, among others, figures like these are often attributed—have abandoned here the formulas of the 'great art' in an effort to achieve that natural expression that was much sought after in Christmas crib figures. A humorous, realistic note is struck by the sheep and goats. Skillfully modeled in terra cotta, they are for the most part attributed to Saverio Vassallo, one of the best Neapolitan animaliers of the day.

"The same naturalistic vein appears in the figures of people in the inn of Bethlehem. Here are rich burghers, merchants, or valets, some of which seem to be individual portraits of exhilarating realism, peasants in the gay attire of the islands of Ischia and Procida, or women coming from the countryside to peddle their produce, colorfully displayed in miniature baskets. All of them are potential actors of little genre scenes to be spontaneously set into action and made to relate to one another, in chatter or in laughter, under the sharp limelight of the stage, like the characters of a miniature Commedia dell'Arte.

"The magic of the theater and the warmth of simple, sincere emotions are still today the most endearing qualities of a Neapolitan crèche."

III / *After a magnificent display during the holiday season, what is done about the "care and feeding" of these small wonders for the rest of the year? As each figure is taken from the tree, it is dusted with a soft sable brush. Then it is carefully examined to determine whether it should go directly to the Museum's vast temperature-controlled storage rooms, where protective cases hold angels suspended and figures free-standing, or if steps should be taken to preserve the eighteenth-century figures and fabrics.*

Conservation is approached after the most careful consideration and in the most scientific environment. For example, some discoloration was recently found on the lace-trimmed mantle of one of the figures attributed to Lorenzo Mosca. She was sent to the conservation laboratory of the Museum's Costume Institute, and in this nontoxic atmosphere she was photographed from all angles, handled by a conservator wearing cotton gloves. Next, the mantle was removed and a paper pattern was made, fold for fold, so that the original could be refolded exactly. Special photographs were taken with a special camera attached to a microscope, and a minute specimen of fiber was analyzed to see if any attempt should be made to remove the stain. The decision was made to try a water method. The tiny mantle was taken to the washing table, where nonionic detergent and deionized water were gently applied. It was then put on the drying table and very lightly finger-pressed and refolded. Had it been decided that the fabric could not stand up to a water washing, it would probably have been dusted with a very absorbent powder and vacuumed with an aspirator to withdraw the stain.

If the figure's terra-cotta head or wooden hands and feet had needed some attention, she would have been sent to Objects Conservation. There, even with the help of special cameras, an x-ray machine, and a chemistry laboratory, it is the eye, the hand, the human judgment that tells the conservator just how far to go. A broken finger or hand would be seen by a wood specialist, who might find that hide glue would be enough to rejoin the pieces—a repair that could be reversed at a later

date if necessary. If the pieces needed more support, a tiny pin would be inserted. If paint was flaking, a sample would be viewed in a scanning electron microscope, which magnifies up to four hundred thousand times, to determine its contents and condition; then a decision would be made on how to restore its patination. In the eighteenth century, after the little head was sculptured and fired, it was covered with a white gesso, polychromed with tempera, and polished to a high sheen. To restore this effect might be a matter of injecting gelatin and a fungicide between the terra cotta and the raised gesso, and lightly pressing the gesso back into place. If there was a greater loss, it would be isolated with a synthetic resin so that the fill could be removed later at the discretion of a future curator and conservator. The new white gesso fill, a mixture of whiting, hide glue, and water, similar to the recipe used in the eighteenth century, would be polychromed with a gouache pigment and varnished with a synthetic resin to duplicate the luster.

IV / At the Metropolitan in late autumn, there is a ripple of excitement when the center of the Medieval Hall is closed off with gray work screens. Staff and visitors know that this is the beginning of the great Christmas tree, and they plan their walks to watch its progress. Surprisingly enough, it starts from the top. A thirty-foot pole is inserted into a sculptured wooden base that has been put together like a giant jigsaw puzzle. The highest part goes up first, complete with star, branches, and the two topmost angels. For the next few weeks the tree grows down instead of up, branch by branch, angel by angel, until it reaches its fullest point and is surrounded by a modeled landscape and architectural elements. During the last week the crèche figures are arranged in a composition that changes from year to year as figures are added and the setting is redesigned to accept them. Miniature handmade plants and flowers and real moss are added. The lighting is refined, the music rehearsed, and all is ready for the opening night.

The installation of the crèche is the result of years of collaboration between Loretta Howard and a number of noted artists, architects, and set and lighting designers. The artist Enrique Espinoza, who has worked on the tree from the beginning, designed the dazzling star at the top. The Museum's electricians, carpenters, riggers, and painters are the indispensable supporting team. Children, grandchildren, and friends of the family have all participated. For Loretta Howard, the annual recreation of the angel tree was an act of love and religious devotion.

After attending a lighting of the tree, Diana Loercher of the <u>Christian Science Monitor</u> wrote this account: "It is an exalted and exalting tree, very much at home in the solemn sculpture hall. As the organ played 'Silent Night' at dusk, a large crowd of children and adults gazed expectantly upward. First the star began to glow, then a light appeared over the crèche, then the candles shone, and finally the spotlights illuminated the angels.

"It was a crescendo of light, like sun breaking through the clouds, and the audience responded with soft gasps. I asked one little girl, who turned out to be Mrs. Howard's granddaughter, what she liked best about the ceremony. She replied, 'I like best to watch my grandmother's face.' It is a face that lights up with the tree."

"He shall give His angels charge over thee," said the Psalmist. One feels the presence of angels as one rejoices in the radiance and beauty of Loretta Howard's angel tree.

THE NATIVITY

*And she brought forth her firstborn son, and wrapped him
in swaddling clothes, and laid him in a manger; because there
was no room for them in the inn.*

*And there were in the same country shepherds abiding in
the field, keeping watch over their flock by night.*

*And, lo, the angel of the Lord came upon them, and the glory
of the Lord shone round about them: and they were sore afraid.*

*And the angel said unto them, Fear not: for, behold,
I bring you good tidings of great joy, which shall
be to all people.*

*For unto you is born this day in the city of David a Saviour,
which is Christ the Lord.*

*And this shall be a sign unto you; Ye shall find the babe
wrapped in swaddling clothes, lying in a manger.*

*And suddenly there was with the angel a multitude of the
heavenly host praising God, and saying,*

*Glory to God in the highest, and on earth peace, good will
toward men.*

LUKE 2:7–14

Now when Jesus was born in Bethlehem of Judæa in the days of Herod the king, behold, there came wise men from the east to Jerusalem,

Saying, Where is he that is born King of the Jews? for we have seen his star in the east, and are come to worship him.

When they had heard the king, they departed; and, lo, the star, which they saw in the east, went before them, till it came and stood over where the young child was.

When they saw the star, they rejoiced with exceeding great joy.

And when they were come into the house, they saw the young child with Mary his mother, and fell down, and worshipped him: and when they had opened their treasures, they presented unto him gifts; gold, and frankincense, and myrrh.

MATTHEW 2:1 − 2, 9 − 11

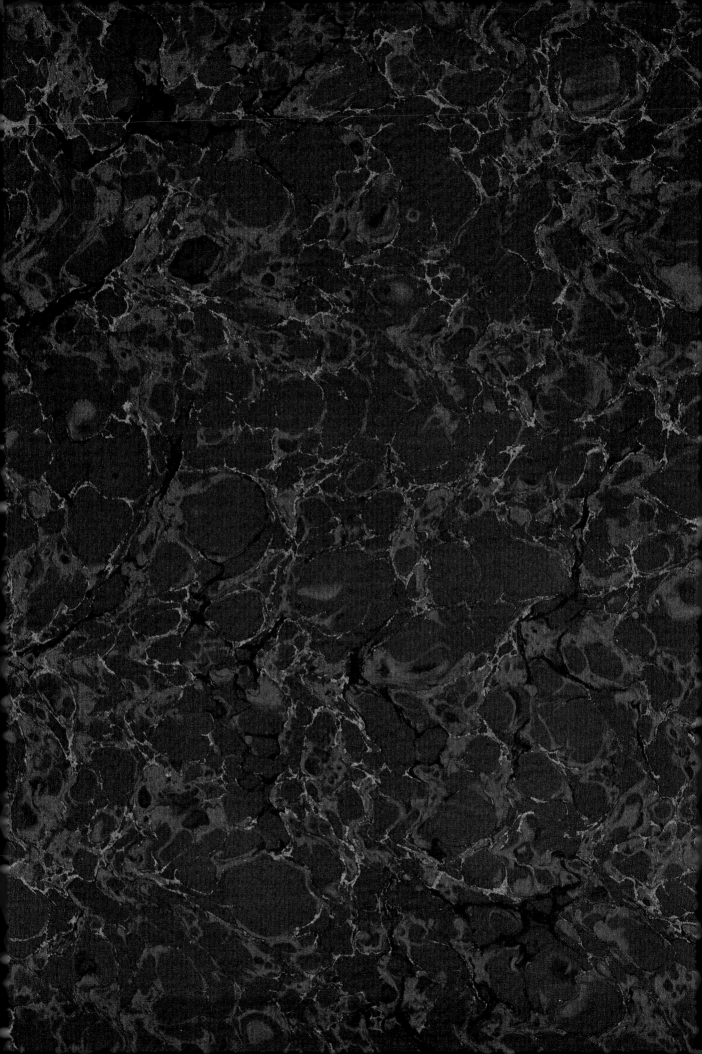

"Behold, I bring you good tidings of great joy..." LUKE 2:10

"The Son of man shall send forth his angels..." MATTHEW 13:41

"The Lord…will send his angel with thee, and prosper thy way…" GENESIS 24:40

While the faces of the people in this Neapolitan panorama
are realistic, the faces of the angels are artists' depictions
of faces celestial. According to the scriptures of many
religions, angels are God's messengers carrying his thoughts
to man: announcing, proclaiming, guiding, guarding,
lighting the way. Angels bring spiritual ideas, the gift
of inspiration; they infuse hearts with love. Artists of
eighteenth-century Italy sculptured each little angel's head
in terra cotta, with exquisite care, emotion, and finesse
—parted lips, rounded cheeks, eyes filled with wonder.
Their expressions are of joy, rapture, exaltation. The
carved and painted wings, the graceful hands, the flowing
hair and drapery are a triumph of baroque splendor.

"There is joy in the presence of the angels..." LUKE 15:10

"If I take the wings of the morning, and dwell in the uttermost parts of the sea; Even there

shall thy hand lead me…" PSALMS 139:9–10

All come to see Him: the townsmen, the shepherds

of the field, the Kings from afar. The wise men and

their retinues are dressed in the splendor of the eighteenth-

century Neapolitan courts. Their glittering clothes are made

of rustling silks, taffetas, brocades, velvets; encrusted with

silver and gold metallic braids and fringes; splashed with

sequins and pearls. Twisted turbans are topped with golden

crowns. Sparkling earrings, pendants, and belts, made by

the famous goldsmiths and silversmiths of that day,

shimmer in the light. Golden daggers, scimitars, and silver

filigree baskets bear the hallmarks of their makers.

All come to pay homage, led by the star.

"Give unto the Lord the glory due unto his name.." PSALMS 96:8

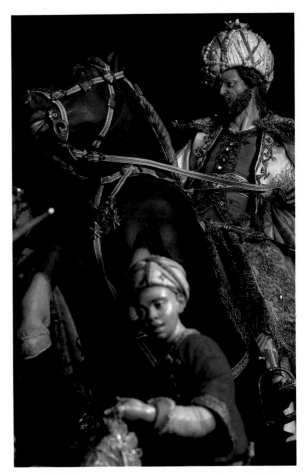

"It is God that girdeth me with strength, and maketh my way perfect." PSALMS 18:32

"O Lord, how manifold are thy works! in wisdom hast thou made them all: the earth is full

of thy riches." PSALMS 104:24

"*For with thee is the fountain of life: in thy light shall we see light.*" PSALMS 36:9

"O sing unto the Lord a new song: sing unto the Lord, all the earth....
Honour and majesty are before him: strength and
beauty are in his sanctuary." PSALMS 96:1,6

Eighteenth-century Neapolitan crèche settings surrounded
the Holy Family with scenes of local life — town people
and country people offering as gifts the wares of their trades,
all reflecting the excitement of the happening. Olga Raggio
refers to them as "potential actors of little genre scenes…
under the sharp limelight of the stage, like the characters
of a miniature Commedia dell'Arte."

The crèche is theatre, and a crèche maker must be a director
who sees to the actors, the sets, the costumes, the lights,
the music. The production is lavish. Tree and landscape
must be adjusted to receive each addition to the collection.
Hills, rocks, shrubs, houses, walls, steps, and other architectural elements must be constructed, painted, and antiqued.

There is special lighting for the face of each figure and a
generous sprinkling of candles to create a certain glow. Scores
of small lights in the star shine forth as silver and golden rays.
Finally, the angel tree is bathed in a soft, warm light from above.

"For the son of man shall come in the glory of his Father with his angels..." MATTHEW 16:27

"Music is well said to be the speech of angels," wrote Goethe. Much has been written about angels and music. Matthew said: "And he shall send his angels with a great sound of a trumpet" (24:31). In "The Angels' Song," written by Edmund Hamilton Sears in 1850, you feel the closeness of angels and music:

It came upon the midnight clear,
  That glorious song of old,
From Angels bending near the earth
  To touch their harps of gold;

"Peace on the earth, good will to men
  From Heaven's all gracious King."
The world in solemn stillness lay
  To hear the angels sing.

The following words by Marion Susan Campbell are set to a seventeenth-century melody:

Angels at the Saviour's birth
  Woke with music all the earth.

Still the tidings angels bring
  With their joyful caroling.

Feeling that music is an important part of the theatre of the crèche, Loretta Howard enveloped the angel tree in sublime Christmas music. Visitors step into an atmosphere of visual wonder and "hear the angels sing."

"The heavens declare the glory of God..." PSALMS 19:1

"Thy righteousness is like the great mountains; thy judgments are a great deep: O Lord, thou preservest man and beast." PSALMS 36:6

"...and a little child shall lead them." ISAIAH 11:6

"…rejoice in his light." JOHN 5:35

"Be still, and know that I am God..." PSALMS 46:10

"The angel of the Lord descended from heaven..." MATTHEW 28:2

The angels are so graceful, they remind one of ballet dancers. The positions and movements of the fifty figures are choreographed with great care. They seem to pivot and swirl — always in the direction of the crib. Tiny swivels in the hidden rods that suspend the angels around the tree allow them to be moved from side to side and backward and forward. Arms, legs, wings — all are flexible, so each angel assumes an individual attitude.

The angels circle and edge the tree to dramatize its great silhouette, skimming the surface as if in flight. Their silken robes, hemmed with fine wire so they can be shaped in different ways, have a sense of being caught in the breeze of fluttering wings. The angels look alive, in motion — never still. Drawn by the radiance, each one turns toward the Holy Babe.

A small child came to see the angel tree, and after looking about with much wonder she said: "Mommy, why are the angels dressed in rags?" Loretta Howard overheard this and decided it was time to take some of the angels out of their original clothes, now pale and shredded beyond conservation. She searched for antique silks still in glorious color and meticulously re-created the angel costumes.

Just as each head is a sculpted portrait, each costume is designed for its figure and distinguishes it from all the others. People often refer to a particular angel by its dress—the angel with the crimson mantle, the angel in the orchid robe. The museum reference card for one of the angels attributed to Salvatore di Franco includes this description: "Angel with windblown, brown hair, in white robe, yellow mantle, green scapular with gold brocade belt, blue and pink tipped wings." These colorful compositions of floating silks, polychromed wood, and terra cotta restore to the angels the glory and beauty of their youth.

"He hath made every thing beautiful..." ECCLESIASTES 3:11

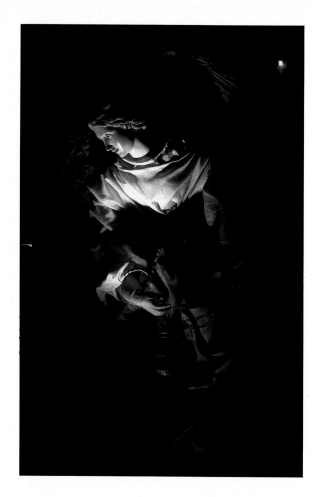

"Praise ye him, all his angels: praise ye him, all his hosts." PSALMS 148:2

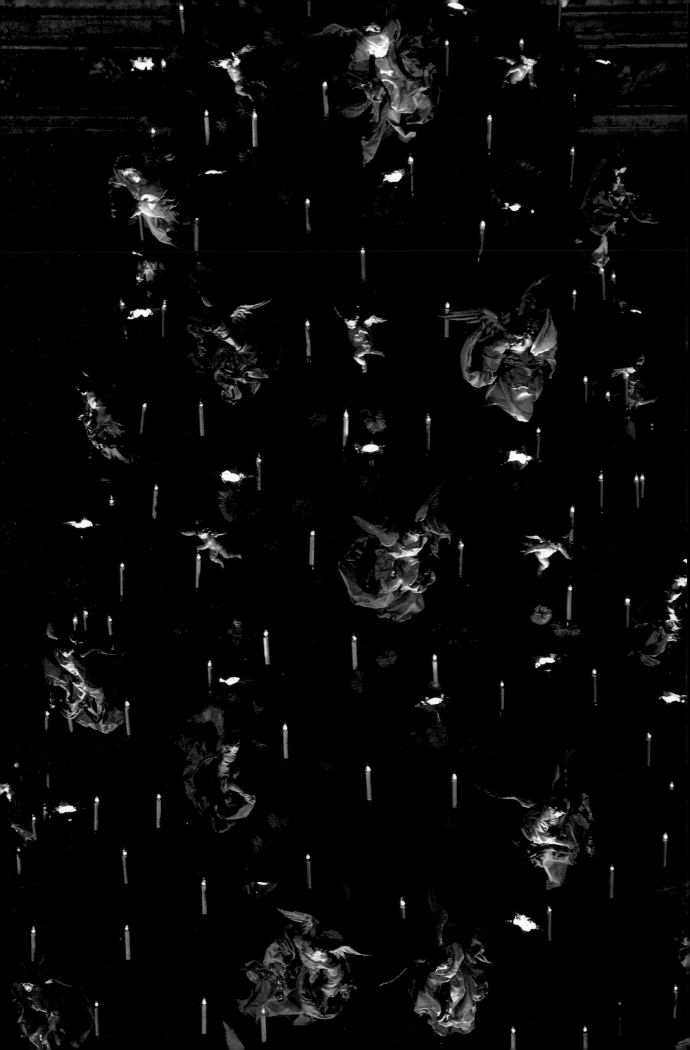

A T T R I B U T I O N S

Traditional attributions of some of the figures to known Neapolitan artists:

MATTEO BOTTIGHERI
Woman with basket, page 37

FRANCESCO CELEBRANO
Terra-cotta angel, page 23

SALVATORE DI FRANCO
Angel, page 26 (top)

Angel, page 28

Mary and Joseph, page 56

Angel, page 58 (lower center)

Angel, page 63

Angel, pages 66–67

FRANCESCO GALLO
Young bull, page 41

GIUSEPPE GORI
King's attendant, page 34

Lady, page 40

Cherubs, page 48

Angel, page 64 (lower left)

NICOLA INGALDI
King, page 33 (lower left)

LORENZO MOSCA
Angel, page 29

Angel, page 69

GIUSEPPE SAMMARTINO
The Infant, page 56

Angels, page 62

Angel, page 65

Angel, page 71 (left)

A VASSALLO BROTHER
Sheep, page 39 (lower right)

Loretta Howard documented so well the development of the Christmas crèche exhibit at the Metropolitan in albums of newspaper and magazine articles, personal letters, and manuscripts of her lectures. These albums, and her extensive collection of books about crèches, have been a great help to us in preparing our text. She was most kind and patient answering our many questions. She attended the first photographic sitting and was delighted with the results.

The staff of the Metropolitan Museum showed their appreciation of Loretta Howard's work and their interest in this book in many ways. We want to thank especially Philippe de Montebello for his very gracious foreword. Bradford Kelleher and Lisa Cook Koch gave us a most enthusiastic go-ahead. Olga Raggio and Johanna Hecht generously shared their scholarly knowledge and resources. Richard Morsches, in charge of Museum operations, the person to whom Loretta Howard often turned, helped us to trace the evolution of the tree. Interviews with Peter Fischer, Judith Jerde, John Canonico, and Ann Luce revealed much about the construction of the tree and the conservation of the crèche figures. During our photographic sittings we were aided by Franz Schmidt and his able staff, and the Museum's security personnel.

To perpetuate the tree for the enjoyment of future generations, Loretta Howard established a permanent Christmas Tree Fund. Ashton Hawkins guided a plan to augment the fund to support the publication of this book in her memory. We want to thank him, and to thank William B. Macomber, who wrote the very warm letter to friends of Loretta Howard that brought such a wonderful response. We are most grateful to Tadeusz Adamowski, Margaret and Joseph Bafford, Marie Bauer, Glenn Boocock, James Borynack, Josephine Brune, Silas Cathcart, Orrin Christy, Harriet Clay, Bradley Collins, Louise Connell, Rita and Allerton Cushman, Catherine Dewey, John Diserio, Bertha Donahue, Bishop John J. Dougherty, Nancy Carrol-Draper, Noreen and Dow Drukker, Reverend Mother Benedict Duss, Sylvia French, Evelyn Gates, Gerard George, Jacqueline and Yves Gonnet, Carol Gourley, David Granger, Susan and Anthony Gristina, Kathryn and Erik Hanson, Barbara Hines, Florence Hines, Marcia and Edward Hines, Joan Hinken, Dagney Holland-Martin, Lynn Howard, Mimi and Howell Howard, Catherine and David Hume, Katherine Hurd,

ACKNOWLEDGMENTS

Seymour Knox, Louise Levenson, Fernando Losada, Suzanne Maclear, Electra and Fletcher McDowell, Harriet and Melvin McGee, Everard Meade, Eric Miller, Helen Miller, Anne and Robert Model, Elizabeth Moore, Edwina Otis, Helenka Pantaleoni, Nancy Parker, Beverly Pepper, Julie and Werner Pleus, Pauline M. Pollard, Patricia Powell, Hope Williams Read, Loretta Renaker, Dorothy Rowley, The Russian Tea Room, Allan Ryan, Marilyn Salant, Helen Scholz, Andrea Selby, Christopher Selby, Frederick Selby, Stephanie Selby, Ann and Alan Simpson, Margot Slater, Eloise Spaeth, Louise Stephaich, Jane and George Stern, Missy and Richard Sterne, Eliot Stewart, Faith and James Stewart-Gordon, Linda Sturgis, Loretta and Jack Sturgis, Samuel Swint, Rouben Ter-Arutunian, Constance Terry, Phyllis Thacker, Margot and Calvin Todd, Joseph Tydings, Joy Ubiña, Harry Van de Ven, Calista Washburn, and Annie Laurie Witzel.

The new tree was made possible by a gift from House & Garden magazine. The sculpted base, designed by architect John Barrington Bayley, was commissioned with monies from two private funds.

We want to thank Miki Denhof for her creative guidance early in the project. Gerard George encouraged us in every way, recalling conversations with Loretta Howard in which she expressed her feelings about her work. Through several interviews with Enrique Espinoza, who was associated so closely with Loretta Howard from the very beginning of the tree, we learned much about how she worked and of her great dedication. Loretta Howard's grandchildren, Christopher, Andrea, and Stephanie Selby, grew up with the tree and told us lovingly of their experiences with their grandmother. Many friends have given us their thoughts and their time: Barbara Annear, Bishop John J. Dougherty, Noreen Drukker, Seymour Knox, Mortimer Laughlin, Alwin Nikolais, Edwina Otis, Hope Williams Read, Susan Roschen, Marianne Ruggeri, Father James Sheilds, Eloise Spaeth, Lyman Stebbins, LeMar Terry, Rouben Ter-Arutunian, Phyllis Thacker, Monsignor Bela Vega. We are most grateful for the immediate enthusiasm and creative direction of Robert Gottlieb, for the guidance and support of our editor Susan Ralston, and for Robert Scudellari's inspired design for the book. All of these people have made the creation of this book an exhilarating and fulfilling experience.

BARZAGHI, ANTONIO. *Il presepe nella cultura de '700 a Napoli.* Treviso, 1983.

BERLINER, RUDOLF. *Die Weihnachtskrippe.* Munich, 1955.

BORRELLI, GENNARO. *Il presepe napoletano.* Rome, 1970.

GOCKERELL, NINA. *The Collection of Cribs in the Bavarian National Museum.* Munich, 1980.

HECHT, JOHANNA. *The Nativity.* New York, 1981.

JOHNSON, SUSAN C. *The Neapolitan Presepio.* Pittsburgh, 1979.

MANCINI, FRANCO. *Il presepe napoletano nella collezione Eugenio Catello.* Florence, 1965.

————. *Il presepe napoletano: scritti e testimonianze dal secolo XVIII al 1955.* Naples, 1983.

PERRONE, ANTONIO. *Historic Notes on the Nativity Scene.* Naples, 1896.

RAGGIO, OLGA. *The Nativity: The Christmas Crèche at the Metropolitan Museum of Art.* New York, 1969.

———— *A Neapolitan Christmas Crèche.* New York, 1976.

ROBECK, NESTA DE. *The Christmas Presepio in Italy.* Florence, 1934.

SPAETH, ELOISE. *Two Eighteenth-century Neapolitan Crèches.* New York, 1961.

SWARZENSKI, HANS. *An Eighteenth-century Crèche.* Boston, 1967.

A NOTE ABOUT THE AUTHORS

Linn Howard assisted her mother, Loretta Hines Howard, with the installation of the tree and crèche at The Metropolitan Museum of Art and now continues her work. She traveled with her mother in Europe on collecting trips and when first married lived in Nepal. She studied art and dancing and was a member of the Alwin Nikolais Company. During the summer season she runs a small dude ranch in Wyoming. The remainder of the year she lives in New York City with her three children, Christopher, Andrea, and Stephanie Selby.

Mary Jane Pool has a special interest in eighteenth-century Italian decorative arts and collects furniture painted in that period. She is on the board of the Isabel O'Neil Foundation for the Art of the Painted Finish and is a governor of the Decorative Arts Trust. From 1970 to 1980 she was Editor in Chief of House & Garden magazine. She has edited several books, including Billy Baldwin Decorates and Twentieth Century Decorating, Architecture & Gardens.

Elliott Erwitt's interest in photography was born while he was a teenager living in Hollywood. Since 1948 his work has appeared, both as illustrations and in advertisements, in virtually every European and American popular magazine and has been exhibited in many galleries and museums in the United States, Europe, and Japan. His books include Photographs and Anti-Photographs, Son of Bitch, Observations on American Architecture, and Recent Developments. He has been a member of Magnum Photos, the international photographers' cooperative, since 1953.